Why Do Cats Have Whiskers?

With lots of love to Tiger, Goldie, Charlena, Blur, Jin-Jin, Noir, Pewter, Sacha, Jerry, Jewel, Tonya, Gus, Smedley and _____ (add the name of your cat here)—LM

Why Do Cats Have Whiskers?

By Elizabeth MacLeod

Kids Can Press

Kids Can Press acknowledges the financial support of the Government of Ontario, through the Ontario Media Development Corporation's Ontario Book Initiative; the Ontario Arts Council; the Canada Council for the Arts; and the Government of Canada, through the BPIDP, for our publishing activity.

Published in Canada by	Published in the U.S. by
Kids Can Press Ltd.	Kids Can Press Ltd.
29 Birch Avenue	2250 Military Road
Toronto, ON M4V 1E2	Tonawanda, NY 14150

www.kidscanpress.com

Edited by Karen Li
Designed by Marie Bartholomew
Printed and bound in China

Photo Credits

p. 6: © istockphoto.com/Vladimir Suponev; p. 8 (t): Asten Rathbun; p. 10: © istockphoto.com/Tracy Scott-Murray; p. 12: © istockphoto.com/Paul Senyszyn; p. 14 (t): Rachel Freedman; p. 15 (t), 19: Peter Mintz Photographer; p. 20: Adrienne Tang; p. 21, 23: © istockphoto.com/Eric Isselée; p. 22 (Birman): George Doyle & Ciaran/Stockbyte/Getty Images, (Cornish Rex): Purestock; p. 23 (Japanese Bobtail): Kathleen M. Grone, (Ocicat): Carolyn A. McKeone, (Siberian): Michael Huettl, (Persian): © istockphoto.com/Cathy Keifer; p. 25: © istockphoto.com/ThePropShoppe; p. 26 (b): © istockphoto.com/Vladimir Suponev; p. 30: George Doyle & Ciaran/Stockbyte/Getty Images; p. 32: © istockphoto.com/Lars Christensen; p. 33 (b): © istockphoto.com/Eric Isselée; p. 34: © istockphoto.com/Nancy Louie; p. 36: © istockphoto.com/Denis Tabler; p. 38, 41: Marisa D'Andrea; p. 43: Marc DuBoisson; p. 45: © istockphoto.com/Edzard de Ranitz; p. 46 (t): Rachel Rogosin; p. 48 (t): Judy Brunsek; p. 49: © istockphoto.com/Nikolai Okhitin; p. 51: © istockphoto.com/Marek Tihelka; p. 50: © istockphoto.com/Nikita Tiunov; p. 54: © istockphoto.com/Vladimir Suponev; p. 57: Miriam Barry; p. 59: © istockphoto.com/Andreea Manciu.

All other photos Photodisc Inc. Stockbyte, JUPITERIMAGES.

Many thanks to consultant Dr. Greg Usher, Usher Animal Hospital, Toronto, Ontario

This book is smyth sewn casebound.

CM 08 0 9 8 7 6 5 4 3 2 1

Library and Archives Canada Cataloguing in Publication

MacLeod, Elizabeth

   Why do cats have whiskers? / Elizabeth MacLeod.

ISBN 978-1-55453-196-7

 1. Cats—Juvenile literature. I. Title.

SF445.7.M32 2008   j636.8   C2007-905251-7

Kids Can Press is a *corus*™ Entertainment company

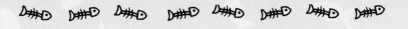

Contents

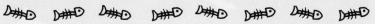

Chapter 1

When Cats Were Gods

Cats have been around for millions of years, first as prehistoric beasts and now as pets. In between, they've been feared and burned, as well as treated as gods.

Humans and cats began their relationship when people realized that cats could work for them and cats discovered humans would feed them. Today, most pet cats are pampered pusses who don't have to earn their dinner. In fact, when you call your cat — Max, Tigger and Smokey are the most popular names — he'll only respond if he feels like it. Why? Some people think it's because he still remembers when his ancestors were gods!

What was the first cat like?

The earliest ancestor of today's cats lived about 30 million years ago. It looked more like a weasel than a cat but had a long tail, large eyes and sharp claws and teeth. Scientists call it *Proailurus*, which means "first cat" in Greek.

The group of animals that pet cats belong to, a group known as "purring cats," finally came along about 12 million years ago.

How big is the biggest wildcat? How small is the smallest?

The biggest wildcat today is the Siberian tiger. It can be more than 3.6 m (12 ft.) long — about as long as a small car — and weigh up to 318 kg (700 lb.).

The Black-footed cat is the smallest wildcat. The females are less than 50 cm (20 in.) long and weigh as little as 1.2 kg (2.5 lb.). Weigh your own cat and see how it compares!

Out of the wild

No one knows for sure how cats moved from the wild into people's homes. It's believed that North African wildcats lived in the bush and grasslands around settlements in Egypt thousands of years ago. Like modern cats, these felines were curious. They may have investigated Egyptian farms and discovered mice and other rodents living in the barns, eating farmers' grain. It probably wasn't long before the cats moved close to the settlements to feed on the mice.

People likely thanked the cats by leaving out food. Cats began to rely on the feedings and sauntered into houses looking for more. These cats stayed and gave birth to kittens. By about 1540 BCE, Egyptian artists were painting scenes of cats in everyday life. One even shows a cat scratching a chair leg!

Did people really worship cats?

Many ancient Egyptians worshiped the goddess Bast, who had a woman's body and a cat's head. (Her name is pronounced Pasht, and the word "pussycat" might come from that name.) Bast's worshipers believed that carved images of cats could protect their families.

In ancient Egypt, killing a cat was a terrible crime that could result in death for the killer. Cats were so loved that their bodies were preserved, or mummified, when they died. Owners shaved off their own eyebrows to show their sorrow. They also included embalmed mice in their cats' tombs so the cats would have food in the afterlife. In the ancient city of Beni Hasan, Egypt, scientists dug up more than 300 000 cat mummies!

Circle, snooze, repeat

Ever noticed how your cat circles around and around before flopping over and falling asleep? This behavior may date back thousands of years when all cats were wild. Back then, cats likely slept in tall grass and before snoozing had to flatten it down to make comfortable nests.

Who's more popular: cats or dogs?

Cats are North America's most popular pets. There are 73 million pet cats, compared to just 63 million pet dogs. About 80 percent of North Americans give their pets presents on their birthdays or for holidays! Do you?

Heavenly cat

Mohammed, one of the most important prophets in the Islamic religion, loved cats. One day, so the legend goes, when Mohammed was called to prayer, he realized that his favorite cat, Muezza, was fast asleep on a sleeve of his robe. Instead of waking Muezza and moving him, Mohammed quietly cut off his sleeve and left to pray.

When Mohammed returned from prayers, Muezza was awake and bowed to his owner to thank Mohammed for not disturbing him earlier. Mohammed stroked his pet three times and guaranteed him a place in heaven.

Another story says that Muezza was a tabby, and Mohammed would often rest his hand on the cat's head. That's why tabby cats today often have an "M" for Mohammed on top of their heads.

How did cats become pets around the world?

Cats were so sacred in ancient Egypt that traders were forbidden to take them away. So sailors and merchants began to smuggle the animals out of Egypt.

Historians believe Mediterranean traders brought cats to Italy by 1000 BCE. It wasn't long before the animals spread throughout Europe, as demand grew for these hunters that preyed on mice and snakes.

When felines reached Japan and China in about 1000 BCE, they were especially welcome. There, rats dined on silkworms and were a threat to the silk industry. Cats quickly became popular predators in Asia.

Vikings probably brought cats with them when they explored North America around the year 1000. In the early 1600s, settlers from England also brought felines to North America.

The Beckoning Cat

Have you ever seen a statue of a
cat with one paw raised? This cat is
called *Maneki Neko*, or the Beckoning
Cat, and it has a long history.

One story about Maneki Neko takes place in
Tokyo, Japan, in the 1600s. A cat named Tama
lived in a temple that had very little money. On
a stormy day, a very powerful lord was riding
by the temple. While taking shelter under a tree,
the nobleman noticed Tama. She was washing
her face with her paw, but the man thought she
was beckoning to him. He walked over to her
and, at that second, the tree he'd been standing
under was struck by lightning. It fell—just
where the lord had been standing.

The man was so grateful
to Tama for saving his life
that he donated money
to the cat's temple.
Tama became a popular
good-luck symbol
and still is today.

Match the Maneki Neko

Maneki Neko statues are modeled after the Japanese Bobtail cat. The color of each statue has a special significance and so does its paw position. Can you pair up the description of each lucky cat with its meaning? (Answers are below.)

1. Right paw raised	a) Warding off evil
2. Left paw raised	b) Money
3. Paw raised high	c) More customers
4. Pink cat	d) Especially good luck
5. Gold cat	e) Good luck
6. Black cat	f) Love
7. Calico (three-colored) cat	g) Good health
8. Red cat	h) Luck from a great distance

Answers: 1. e, 2. c, 3. h, 4. f, 5. b, 6. a, 7. d, 8. g

Famous cat lovers

If you're a cat lover, you're in famous company that includes Albert Einstein, Florence Nightingale, Mark Twain and Queen Victoria. Most people know Isaac Newton was one of the greatest scientists ever. But they don't know that he invented the cat flap. One story says Newton was experimenting in a pitch-black room. Spithead, one of his cats, kept opening the door, wrecking Newton's work. The cat flap kept Newton and Spithead happy.

Have people always loved cats?

Actually, life was very difficult for cats in Europe in the 1200s. Some people thought cats were connected to black magic, and women who owned pet cats were accused of being witches. Many women and their cats were burned alive.

In the mid-1300s, a plague swept across Europe, killing more than half the population. Many people killed cats, thinking they carried the disease. But fleas—and the rats they lived on— were actually the ones carrying the Black Death. So the more cats people killed, the more rats there were to spread the disease.

Soon people realized that cat owners were less likely to get sick—or die—because they had fewer rats in their homes. It wasn't long before cats were again pampered pets.

Black cat superstitions

Whether you think a black cat is lucky or unlucky depends on where you live. In Britain and Australia, black cats are considered lucky. But in many parts of Europe and North America, a black cat crossing your path is thought to bring bad luck. During World War II, American pilots flew Captain Midnight, a black cat, over Germany until he had crossed the path of Nazi leader Adolf Hitler.

But most sailors used to think it was lucky to have a cat on their ships. Even as late as the 1800s, a ship's cargo couldn't be insured unless there was a cat on board!

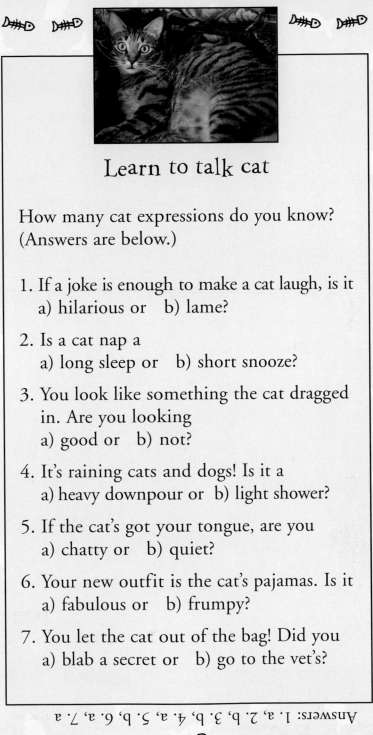

Learn to talk cat

How many cat expressions do you know?
(Answers are below.)

1. If a joke is enough to make a cat laugh, is it
   a) hilarious or   b) lame?

2. Is a cat nap a
   a) long sleep or   b) short snooze?

3. You look like something the cat dragged
   in. Are you looking
   a) good or   b) not?

4. It's raining cats and dogs! Is it a
   a) heavy downpour or b) light shower?

5. If the cat's got your tongue, are you
   a) chatty or   b) quiet?

6. Your new outfit is the cat's pajamas. Is it
   a) fabulous or   b) frumpy?

7. You let the cat out of the bag! Did you
   a) blab a secret or   b) go to the vet's?

Answers: 1. a, 2. b, 3. b, 4. a, 5. b, 6. a, 7. a

Chapter 2

Ragdolls, Scottish Folds and Ocicats

More than 40 breeds of cats are officially recognized at cat shows. As well, there are many more new and developing breeds. Cat breeds have distinct eye and ear shapes, but they differ most in their type of fur.

Most pet cats aren't purebred, or pedigreed, cats. They're known as either Domestic Shorthairs (DSH), Domestic Medium Hairs (DMH) or Domestic Long Hairs (DLH). If one of your pet's features, such as its nose or eyes, makes it look as if one of its parents was pedigreed, some people would call your pet a mixed breed. For a cat to be pedigreed, you have to know all its parents, grandparents and other ancestors.

What are the most popular breeds of cats?

More people own Persian cats than any other pedigreed cat. Also very popular are the Maine Coon cat and the Siamese cat.

Take a tour around the world and meet some of the incredible breeds of cats.

Abyssinian
This Asian breed is famous for its "ticked" coat, which means it has light and dark bands on its fur.

Birman
Striking blue eyes and snowy white paws make this cat from Burma stand out.

Cornish Rex
The unusually short coat of this breed from England lies in waves along its body.

Japanese Bobtail
Shorthaired or longhaired, these cats are known for their short tails.

Scottish Fold
Its folded ears and big round eyes make this cat look like an owl or a teddy bear.

Ocicat
This spotted domestic cat from the United States has been bred to look like a wildcat.

Siamese
This slim cat from Thailand is known for its curiosity and unusual voice.

Persian
This ancient breed from Iran may have fur up to 12.5 cm (5 in.) long.

Siberian
The national cat of Russia has a beautiful thick coat.

Sphynx
The first of these nearly hairless cats was born only about 40 years ago in Canada.

Manx tales

There are plenty of stories to explain how the Manx cat lost its tail. Some say the cat was the last to board Noah's Ark when the whole world was flooded. Like most cats, the Manx wouldn't come when it was called. When it finally arrived, its tail got caught in the door.

Today, a Manx cat with no tail at all is called a "rumpy." If the cat has a little stub of a tail, it's called a "stumpy."

Which pedigreed cat is the smallest? Which is the biggest?

You could hold a Singapura cat in one hand. This smallest breed can weigh just 1.8 kg (4 lb.) or about as much as five large cans of cat food. Some Maine Coon cats, the largest cat breed, can weigh 11.3 kg (25 lb.). That's almost twice what an average cat weighs.

Why do some Siamese cats look cross-eyed?

In almost all breeds of cats, equal numbers of nerves go from both sides of the brain to each eye. But some Siamese are "cross-wired." These cats inherit a tendency for the nerves from the left side of the brain to go mostly to the right eye. The nerves from the right side of the brain go mostly to the left eye. This causes some double vision, which the cat tries to correct by "crossing" its eyes.

Long ago, people told stories about the Siamese's crossed eyes. One tale tells of a gold cup missing from a temple. Two Siamese cats were sent to find it. When they finally located the cup, the male raced to the temple with the news, while the female guarded the cup. She stared at it so intently she became cross-eyed.

Silky stripes

Stories suggest that the word "tabby" might come from Attabiyah, a neighborhood in Baghdad, Iraq. Here, weavers were long famous for weaving silk with a wavy pattern. Tabbies got their name because their striped coats resembled this special silk. Today, cats with stripy markings are so common that "tabby" has become another word for cat.

Is that cat bald?

Mr. Bigglesworth in the Austin Powers movies really exists — he's a nearly hairless Sphynx! The first one was born in Toronto, Ontario, in 1966.

These cats sometimes seem to act clumsy, just to get a laugh. Most cats with fur have enough hair to absorb their body oils, but Sphynx cats don't and have to be bathed.

Why do cats hate water?

Cat fur doesn't insulate well when it's wet. Most cats love being warm, so it's no wonder that many hate water.

Since most cats like doing things in their own time, on their own terms, they don't like being forced into a bath. But if they get used to it as a kitten, they'll put up with being washed, and some even seem to like it.

The Turkish Van is one pedigreed cat that likes swimming. This ancient breed developed in central Asia. Its coat has a unique thick texture that makes it water-resistant. This cat may take a dip in a swimming pool or try to join its owner in the shower.

Working cats

You'll probably never find a seeing-eye cat or sled cat. A cat just doesn't have the personality for that kind of work. But some cats work with law enforcers to sniff out smuggled fish. Others walk tightropes and ride bikes in circuses. There's even a cat that gives piano concerts!

Many cats hunt mice in shops or stables. Ninety the cat kept rats from chewing the plans for a bridge across the Connecticut River. He led the parade when the bridge opened.

There are therapy cats that visit hospitals and nursing homes. Touching these cats or hearing them purr makes people feel better. One cat had an "out-of-this-world" job. In 1963, France sent Felix the cat skyward in a rocket, making him the first cat in space.

Practice makes purr-fect

With patience and some healthy cat treats, you can teach your cat tricks.

Start with "shaking a paw." Sit in front of your cat, touch one of his front paws and say, "Shake." When your cat lifts his paw, shake it, then praise your cat and give him a treat.

You can also teach your cat to wave. Hold a treat in front of his nose, just out of reach. Move your hand back and forth and tell your cat to wave. Your cat will seem to wave as he reaches for the food. Praise and reward him.

Remember:

- Work on just one trick at a time.

- Repeat a command the same way every time.

- Praise your cat when he does anything right.

Ancient breed

The Egyptian Mau is probably the oldest breed of cat. These are the cats that you see in ancient Egyptian artwork and likely the felines that those long-ago people treated as gods. The breed is so ancient that its name, Mau, is the Egyptian word for cat.

Modern cat lovers have bred other spotted cats, but Maus are the only naturally spotted breed of domestic cat. They are smart and loyal and known for their sweet, almost musical voices and graceful walk. No wonder the ancient Egyptians worshiped them!

My cat has orange stripes and a white chest — what breed is it?

Most pet cats are not pedigreed and are known as DSH, DMH or DLH (see page 21). Pedigreed or not, felines come in combinations of three basic colors: black, white and red (orange). These colors may be pale, or dilute, which results in brown or gray cats, for instance. A black, white and red cat is a tri-color. The colors can be in blocks (known as calico) or woven together (tortoiseshell).

A cat's fur may be solid-colored or patterned. Tabby cat patterns, for instance, include stripes, whorls or spots. A striped tabby is known as "tiger" or "mackerel." If it has a white bib or boots, make that "tabby with white."

So you might say your orange-and-white house cat is a red with white mackerel tabby DSH. Sounds impressive, doesn't it?

What's the most expensive cat ever?

If you want to buy an unusual breed of cat, it may cost you as much as $3500. Why is a pedigreed cat so expensive? A lot of work goes into creating breeds, and most breeders give their cats only the highest-priced food and care.

The most expensive cat ever purchased was a California Spangled cat. It was sold to an anonymous movie star for $24 000! These rare cats have a spotted, or "spangled," tabby coat and a long body. Owning one is like having a pet leopard.

You might say one of the costliest cats ever is Little Nicky. He cost his owner $50 000! Little Nicky is a clone, or exact copy, of an older cat, and the technology that created him is still very expensive.

Pampered pussycats

Long ago, Burmese cats were only
owned by royalty and priests in
Burma (now Myanmar). Legends
say that every aristo-cat had its
own servant, while the temple cats belonged
to monks-in-training who had to cater to the
animals' every whim. Burmese owners today
say these cats still expect royal treatment!

What's so funny?

With its thick, gray-blue coat and golden eyes,
the Chartreux (you say it shar-TRUH) from
France is a handsome breed of cat.
But it's most famous for its smile.
Because of the Chartreux's rounded
forehead and long, narrow muzzle,
these cats always seem to
be smiling.

Siamese stories

Many legends have grown up around the Siamese cat's distinctive dark paws, ears and nose. Breeders call these areas "points," but in Thai legends they're known as "the shadow of the ancient gods' hands." One story claims a pale-colored cat so pleased a deity that he picked it up and stroked it. The places where the god touched the cat were blessed and turned dark.

The color of the points is actually related to heat: the cool areas are darkest. Siamese kittens are born all white. The warmth they experience inside their mother's body keeps the points from darkening for a few weeks.

Which cat is that?

Find out how much you know about the various breeds of cats by matching the breed below to its characteristic. Want to see what some of these amazing cats look like? Ask an adult to help you check the Web for photos and more information. (Answers are below.)

Breed	Characteristic
1. Ragdoll	a) Fur in ringlets and a curly tail
2. Scottish Fold	b) Looks like the black leopards of India
3. Pixie-Bob	c) Gray-blue fur
4. American Curl	d) Has folded ears
5. American Wirehair	e) Resembles a wild bobcat
6. LaPerm	f) Ears curl back in a graceful curve
7. Russian Blue	g) Spotted coat like an ocelot
8. Havana Brown	h) Relaxes completely in your arms
9. Ocicat	i) Chocolate-brown fur
10. Bombay	j) Crimped whiskers and a coarse coat

Answers: 1. h, 2. d, 3. e, 4. f, 5. j, 6. a, 7. c, 8. i, 9. g, 10. b

Chapter 3

The Nose Knows

Deep down, even pampered indoor cats
are hunters, and their bodies have developed
to make them excellent predators. A cat's
nose, ears and eyes are all supersensitive. For
instance, its vision is 10 times sharper than
yours, and a cat can sense 200 million
different smells. Cats are built to explore,
hunt, balance — and even predict weather!

Why do cats have whiskers?

On either side of a cat's nose are vital tools: whiskers. A cat usually has about 12 whiskers on each side of its face, arranged in rows. A cat also has whiskers on many other parts of its face, as well as on the backs of its front legs.

These thick, supersensitive hairs help a cat calculate the width of any passage so that the animal can decide if it can squeeze through. Whiskers also protect the cat's eyes, since the hairs trigger the cat to blink if something touches them.

Whiskers sense air currents around objects such as trees or furniture. They also act as wind detectors to pinpoint the source of a smell. That's handy if you're stalking prey in the dark. Some people think a cat's whiskers can even pick up air vibrations that signal weather changes.

Whiskers can give a cat's *owner* messages, too. If your cat wants cuddling, her whiskers are probably curved forward. If your cat is irritated, her whiskers will point back.

Which animal can hear better: a cat or a dog?

Cats can hear better than most animals—better than dogs and much better than you. Cats hear high-pitched noises especially well—that's why they're so good at locating mice and other tiny prey—but their ears are less sensitive to very low sounds. Perhaps that explains why some cats respond better to female voices than to male voices.

In each of a cat's ears are 32 muscles—you only have 6. All of that muscle power lets the cat pivot each ear separately and swivel them around so far that the cat can hear in every direction without moving its head.

Undercover cats

The time: November 1964.
The place: Holland's embassy in Moscow, Russia.

Staff there noticed that the embassy's two Siamese cats kept meowing and clawing at the walls of the building. Their owners finally investigated, expecting to find mice. Instead, they discovered microphones hidden by Russian spies!

When the mikes were turned on, they made a very quiet sound—too quiet for humans to hear. Luckily, the two Siamese had typical supersensitive feline hearing.

Why do cats have fur in their ears?

A cat's ear fur keeps dust and dirt out of the inner ears, helps direct sounds into the ears and insulates the ears when temperatures drop. Did you know that the tufts of hair in a cat's ears are called "ear furnishings"?

Homeward bound

Scientists call it "psi-trailing," but cat owners call it incredible. Cats have a fantastic ability to find their way home, even if it means traveling great distances. For instance, shortly after a cat named Ninja moved with his family from Utah to Washington, he disappeared. About a year later, Ninja turned up at the old house, more than 1365 km (850 mi.) away!

A tabby named Cindy went missing when the house of her owner, Brenda James, was robbed. Brenda moved away — and Cindy turned up at the new house two years later.

Some experts think cats use the angle of the sunlight to find their way. Others believe cats have magnetized cells in their brains that act like compasses. But no one knows how cats find homes they've never even visited.

Do cats have nine lives?

People have long been amazed at a cat's ability to survive falls from great heights. This animal's highly developed inner ear gives it fantastic balance. As well, a cat is flexible enough to twist around and land on all four feet. No wonder people say cats have nine lives.

Shakin' all over

Some researchers believe that cats and other animals can predict earthquakes. These scientists collect stories of cats that run away from home, as well as cats that hiss crazily or slink nervously or just before a quake strikes.

Some seismologists, or earthquake experts, believe that changes in the earth's gravity before an earthquake move a magnetic mineral in cats' bodies. Other researchers think that cats and other animals pick up radio signals emitted from the ground just before an earthquake.

Furry forecasters

Some people think cats can predict the weather. They believe, for instance, that if a cat licks itself, a storm will come soon. That makes sense, scientifically. Just before a storm, the air is full of electricity, which makes a cat's dry fur attract dust. By grooming, the cat dampens and cleans its fur.

Watch your cat for the actions listed below. Then check the weather. How good a forecaster is your feline?

- If a cat keeps looking out a window, rain will fall.
- If a cat lies with its paws stretched out in front, bad storms are near.
- A cat sleeping with its paws tucked under it means cold weather is coming.

Why do cats walk the way they do?

Most animals walk by moving alternate legs — right, left, right, left is their pattern. Only a few move the front and back legs on one side first and then the front and back legs on the other — right, right, left, left. These animals include giraffes, camels — and cats. This "pacing" saves energy and ensures speed and agility.

Why do cats scratch furniture?

Cats scratch to keep their claws sharp. Scratching removes covers that grow over the claws — you'll sometimes find these sheaths around your home.

Another way cats keep their claws sharp is by retracting them when they walk so the claws don't get worn down. Cats are the only animals that can do this!

Multi-toes

Most cats have 5 toes on each front paw and 4 on each back paw, for a total of 18 toes. But some cats have 6 or 7 toes per paw. The record-holding cat for most toes is Jake of Bonfield, Ontario, with 28! Many-toed felines are called polydactyl cats, and sometimes their paws look like mittens.

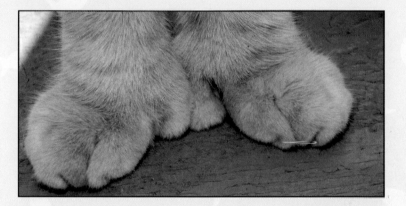

No-skid paws

A cat can jump more than five times its height straight up into the air! Cats won't skid when they land because they have a special pad on each paw that's just behind and above the other pads. And just as you can be right-handed or left-handed, a cat can be right- or left-pawed.

Can cats see in the dark?

Cats can't see in complete darkness, but their eyes are built to see well just before dawn and just after dusk, which are the best hunting times. These predators only need one-sixth of the light that we do, for two reasons.

First, their pupils are built to open fully in dim light, allowing in a maximum amount of light. As well, a cat's eye contains a layer of cells that reflects light and so makes more use of it. This layer, the tapetum, is what makes cat's eyes sometimes glow at night.

Felines also have good 3-D vision and can focus quickly on fast-moving objects. When a cat chases its prey, it keeps its head level — dogs and humans bob their heads up and down.

How shocking!

Ever pet your cat, only to have you both jump when sparks fly between you? That shocking experience is due to weather and how your cat's fur reacts to electricity.

When the air is dry, as it tends to be in winter or when the weather is fair, your cat's fur becomes charged with static electricity. That's the same electricity that sends sparks when you're wearing socks and you shuffle across a carpet. As your pet licks itself, the moisture makes it easier for the electricity to "leak" off the fur. You pet your cat—ZAP!

On a dry day, try petting your cat in a dark room and see if you can spot any sparks.

How old is your cat?

If you know how old your cat is, you can calculate its age in human years. Many cats live to be 20 — about 93 in human years — and some live more than 30 years. Use this chart to calculate how old your cat is in human years.

Cat Age	Human Age
3 months	5 years
6 months	10 years
1 year	15 years
2 years	24 years
3 years	28 years
4 years	32 years
5 years	36 years
6 years	40 years
7 years	44 years
8 years	48 years
9 years	52 years
10 years	56 years
12 years	64 years
14 years	72 years
16 years	81 years
18 years	90 years
20 years	93 years

Why do cats drink so noisily?

Most animals suck up water, but cats noisily lap it up. A cat takes four or five laps for every time it swallows. Unlike your tongue, a cat's tongue curls down and under when the cat drinks. This lets it hold its eyes up to keep watch while it drinks.

Crazy for catnip!

About half of all cats go crazy for catnip — even the smell of it drives them wild. Domestic cats aren't the only felines who react to catnip. Lions and tigers do, too.

Experts think that what excites cats is an oil in the catnip known as nepetalactone. Researchers believe this substance reminds cats of a female cat chemical, or hormone.

How come my cat sleeps so much?

Cats sleep up to 18 hours every day, more than any other animal! They sleep so much because they don't get a lot of deep sleep. For more than half of their snoozing time, they're only in light sleep. This way they're always on alert and can wake up quickly.

Good to the last dropping

The world's rarest coffee, *Kopi Luwak*, comes from Indonesia, where a wildcat known as a luwak lives. The cat eats coffee berries, and the coffee beans inside pass through its stomach. The beans are harvested from the cats' dung heaps, then cleaned and roasted. Kopi Luwak sells for about $500 per 450 g (1 lb.) bag!

Yuck! What's that?

Scientists call them bezoars, but cat owners call
those slimy, cylindrical masses hairballs. When
a cat licks itself, its rough tongue pulls loose fur
from its coat. If the cat swallows too much fur,
the hair can form a ball that grows in the
stomach until the cat coughs it up.

How to prevent hairballs? Brush your cat often.

Is there anything a cat can't do?

- A cat's jaw can't move sideways, so it can't chew
  large food chunks.
- Cats can't move their front legs out to the side—
  they don't have a true collarbone. But that means
  a cat can squeeze through tiny spaces.
- A cat can't climb headfirst down a tree because
  every claw on a cat's paw points the same way.
  That's why a cat has to back down.

Chapter 4

Cat Chat

Do you talk to your cat? About 95 percent of all cat owners do!

Your cat talks to you, too, but in her own special language. That language includes a lot more than purrs and meows. Your pet sends you messages with the position of her ears, the movement of her tail, a lick of her tongue and more. By watching your cat carefully, you can learn to "speak cat" and get a better idea of what your pet is saying.

Why do cats purr?

Cats purr when they're happy. They also purr when they're threatened or in pain, perhaps to make themselves feel happier or to show submission.

Doctors know that human bones need stimulation to stay strong. Cats may also purr to stimulate, and so strengthen, their bones.

A cat purrs by vibrating its voice box, or larynx, in its throat. To do this, a muscle in the voice box opens and closes the cat's air passage about 25 times every second. As the cat breathes in and out, the combined actions create a purring noise.

Why do cats meow?

Although your cat seems to meow a lot, that's a
noise he reserves for communicating with humans.
A cat almost never meows at another cat. Hissing,
spitting and purring work best with other felines.

Cats have probably learned to change their
meows based on what gets a good reaction from
humans. Short meows sound better to cat
owners than long ones and are more likely to
get a cat what it wants. When your cat gives a
little mew, like a kitten, she's probably coaxing
you to give her a treat.

Do cats only purr and meow?

Cats make about 100 different sounds, while
dogs only make about 10. One of the strangest
sounds your cat may make is a chattering noise
when it sees a bird. Some experts think the cat
is expressing its
frustration at not
being able to catch
the bird, while
others say the cat
is trying to call the
bird closer.

I blink you

Want to tell your cat you love him? Try talking his language. But don't use your mouth; use your eyes. Only try this with a friendly cat that you know well. And if you wear glasses, remove them before you start your "conversation." Some cats see glasses as a wide-eyed stare and feel threatened.

Pick a time when your cat is feeling quiet and happy. Crouch or lie down beside him — the two of you can communicate better if you're on the same level. Your pet probably won't stare at you directly. To him, that's unfriendly. But when you have his attention, blink slowly at him. That says, "I'm happy and relaxed."

If your cat blinks back, you can start a whole blinking conversation. If you're really lucky, he may reach out and nose kiss you.

Why do cats knead?

When your cat was a kitten, he kneaded his paws against his mother as he nursed. Some experts say kneading makes the mother's milk flow faster, while others say the action is one of the first ways a kitten signals that it's happy. Now when your cat is content, he remembers being a full, happy kitten. He kneads as a habit from that time long ago.

Nice to 'ear from you

Should you cuddle your cat when her ears are forward? What about when her ears are flattened to the back?

When a cat is happy, its ears face forward, with a slight tilt toward the back. But if that feline becomes anxious, its ears start to point back and flatten down. If its ears are lying straight back, flat to the cat's head, beware!

If one of the cat's ears is flattened but the other isn't, the cat's trying to figure out how to react. Its ears will pivot around as the cat gathers more information to help it decide what to do. Some owners claim their cats will flick an ear in the direction they are likely to move.

Hero cats

There are many stories of cats that have saved people's lives. Kimberley Kotar of Dorval, Quebec, was in her garden with her cat, Sosa, when a poisonous snake appeared, ready to strike. Sosa attacked the snake, saved Kimberley's life and survived, though bitten in the paw.

Bart belonged to highschooler Jose Ybarra of Illinois. The cat woke up his young owner's mother when the teen was having a life-threatening seizure and so saved Jose's life.

When a burglar broke into the home of Aggie, a cat from Laceyville, Pennsylvania, the feisty feline attacked the robber and drove him away. Would you believe that Aggie is blind?

Sometimes cats get help for themselves. In 1996, Tipper was home alone in Tampa, Florida, when he started choking on his collar. Tipper managed to hit the phone's speed dial, which called 911. Paramedics quickly arrived, removed Tipper's collar and saved his life.

How come my cat cleans herself so much?

A cat doesn't like to leave a trace of where it's been. By regularly licking off old skin and hair with its very rough tongue, a finicky feline leaves behind very little odor for its enemies to detect.

Licking and grooming on a hot day also helps a cat cool down. When a cat licks itself, its saliva evaporates off the fur, which lowers the cat's temperature. Cats don't have sweat glands scattered over their bodies as humans do. Instead, they sweat only through their paws. A hot or nervous cat will leave a trail of little sweaty paw prints.

Tail tales

A cat's tail helps it balance as well as land on its feet if it falls from a great height. It can also help a cat communicate with other cats — and with you. The chart below will let you know what your cat is trying to tell you with just a twitch of his tail.

If my tail is ...	It means ...
Pointing straight up	Hi there!
Tucked in close	I'm nervous.
Smoothly switching	I'm thinking. Hmmm ...
Lashing quickly	Stay away! I'm angry!
Down and fluffed out	I'm scared.

Dig in!

Yuck! Your cat just brought you a dead mouse! Why? She might be bringing you a present or making sure you have fresh food. Or she may be carrying her prey to the place she usually eats or where it's safe from other cats. Your cat might also be trying to teach you how to hunt!

Get off my back!

Hisss! When a cat is feeling threatened, it lets everyone know. The cat arches its back to make itself look as big as possible. Its back is incredibly flexible because it has up to 53 vertebrae, or bones — you only have as many as 34 — and they fit together loosely.

As well, a cat will puff out its fur, turn sideways a little and bristle the hair on its tail, all to make it look bigger. The cat will try to intimidate its enemy by staring at it with wide-open eyes, howling aggressively and not backing down. The cat doesn't want its foe to guess that this angry, spitting animal is actually very frightened.

Why won't my cat behave?

Cats hate being told "No!" If you want to change your cat's behavior, experts agree you'll be much more effective if you praise her good behavior instead of punishing her bad. Cats are independent hunters, and nobody tells them what to do.

If you must scold your cat, only do it when she's in the middle of her bad behavior. Otherwise, she won't know why she's being punished. After a scolding, your cat will likely turn her back on you. She's saying you're top cat and please don't attack her.

Use your cat's name only when you praise her or call her for dinner, never when you're scolding. Make sure she associates her name with only good things.

Head butts

Your cat has a lot of ways of telling you he likes you. A favorite is bumping against you. That usually makes you stroke him, which puts you in contact with the scent glands on his head and lips. These glands leave a faint odor on your hands, and your cat probably likes that smell as much as he likes the pats you're giving him.

Cats also have scent glands under their tails, which is why your pet likes to wind his tail around your leg and why cats sniff under each other's tails.

Mystery communication

Is your cat always at the door waiting for you after school, even if you're sometimes early? Some people tell stories of cats running to the telephone when it rings — but only when their owners are calling. Other cats can sense when their owners are about to have a migraine or seizure. There are also cats that seem to know when a trip to the vet is on the schedule and quickly disappear. No wonder about a third of cat owners think their pets are able to read their minds.

Is it possible that some cats and owners have special ways of communicating? Perhaps. Bats use echolocation to steer, and the "pings" are too high-pitched for humans to hear. Elephants sometimes "talk" using very low tones that humans can't hear. Maybe one day experts will be able to measure the extra-special communication between cats and their owners.